Bee

**Karen Hartley
and
Chris Macro**

Heinemann Library
Des Plaines, Illinois

Published by Heinemann Library,
an imprint of Reed Educational & Professional Publishing,
1350 East Touhy Avenue, Suite 240 West
Des Plaines, IL 60018

Designed by Celia Floyd
Illustrations by Alan Male
Printed in Hong Kong / China

02 01 00 99 98
10 9 8 7 6 5 4 3 2 1

Library of Congress Cataloging-in-Publication Data

Hartley, Karen, 1949-
    Bee / Karen Hartley and Chris Macro.
       p.   cm. -- (Bug books)
    Includes bibliographical references and index.
    Summary: A simple introduction to the physical characteristics, diet, life cycle, predators, habitat, and lifespan of bees.
    ISBN 1-57572-661-0 (lib. bdg.)
    1. Bees--Juvenile literature. [1. Bees.] I. Macro, Chris, 1940-. II. Title. III. Series.
    QL565.2.H368   1998
    595.79'9--dc21
                                        98-4858
                                          CIP
                                          AC

Acknowledgements
The Publishers would like to thank the following for permission to reproduce photographs:
Bruce Coleman: J. Brackenbury p. 10, J. Cancalosi p. 11, J. Shaw p. 21, K. Taylor pp. 8, 12; NHPA: N. Callow p. 28, S. Dalton pp. 4, 13, 16, 17, 18, 19, 20, 26; Oxford Scientific Films: G. Bernard pp. 22, 29, S. Camazine p. 15, G. Dew p. 24, B. Osborne p. 7, R. Packwood p. 6, D. Thompson pp. 5, 9, 14, 23, 27; Premaphotos: K. Preston-Mafham p. 25

Cover photograph reproduced with permission of child: Chris Honeywell; bee: D. Maitland/Telegraph Color Library

Every effort has been made to contact copyright holders of any material reproduced in this book. Any omissions will be rectified in subsequent printings if notice is given to the Publisher.

Any words appearing in the text in bold, **like this**, are explained in the Glossary.

Contents

Where do bees live?

Bumblebees live together in a nest in long grass or underground. Bees choose to live in places where flowers grow, like parks and gardens.

Honeybees live together in a nest
in a **hollow** tree or log. Sometimes
people keep honeybees in a wooden
hive. We are going to look at some
honeybees.

zzzzzzzzzzzzzzzzzzzzzzzzzzzzzzzzzzzzzzzzzzzz

What do bees look like?

Bees have brown and yellow hairs on their bodies. They make the bee's brown and yellow stripes.

All bees have two large eyes which can see up, down, backward, and forward at the same time. They also have three small eyes. They have two **antennae** for touching and smelling.

How big are bees?

Bumblebees, like this one, are about the size of a large grape. Honeybees are about the size of a jellybean. Sometimes their tongues are not long enough to reach the **nectar** in big flowers.

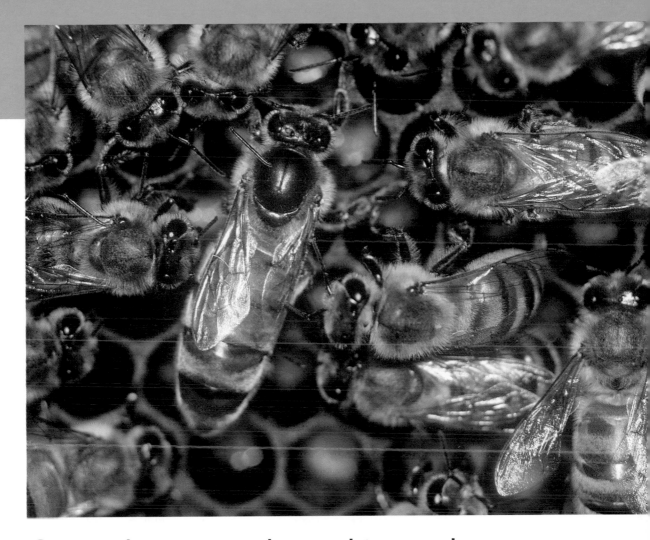

Queen bees are always bigger than worker bees and **drones**. Worker bees are always the smallest kind in the nest. There is only one queen in each nest.

zzzzzzzzzzzzzzzzzzzzzzzzzzzzzzzzzzzz

How are bees born?

In the spring the queen bee **mates** with a **drone**. Then she lays her eggs in special places called cells, inside the nest.

After three days the **larvae hatch** from the eggs. They are small and white. They have no eyes, no legs, and no wings. They are fed by the worker bees.

zzzzzzzzzzzzzzzzzzzzzzzzzzzzzzzzzzzzzzzz

How do bees grow?

After five days the **larvae** turn into **pupae** and begin to turn into adult bees. After two weeks the new bees push off the tops of the cells and crawl out.

The bees' bodies are very soft but they soon get harder. Most of the new bees are worker bees and at first they work inside the nest.

What do bees eat?

Bees eat the **pollen** from flowers. They bring **nectar** from the flowers to the nest to make into honey. They eat the honey in cold weather.

When the **larvae** are in the cells they need to eat to grow. Worker bees feed them honey and pollen.

Which animals attack bees?

Queens and worker bees will **sting** if they are frightened or angry. Their stripes give a warning to other insects not to come near them. Some birds, like the one in the picture, eat bees.

Some worker bees stand at the entrance of the nest to guard it. They will fight bees from other nests if they have come to steal honey.

How do bees move?

All bees have strong wings so they can fly a long way to look for food. When it is hot they fan with their wings to keep the nest cool.

When bees land on a flower they crawl inside it to suck up the **nectar** and collect **pollen**. They wave their **antennae** to help them smell and taste.

How long do bees live?

Queen bees die in the autumn after six or seven years. Princess and worker bees **hibernate** during winter. The worker bees will die next summer after the new workers have **hatched**.

Worker bees push the **drones** out of the nest in the autumn and stop them from coming back in. The drones die because they have no food to eat.

What do bees do?

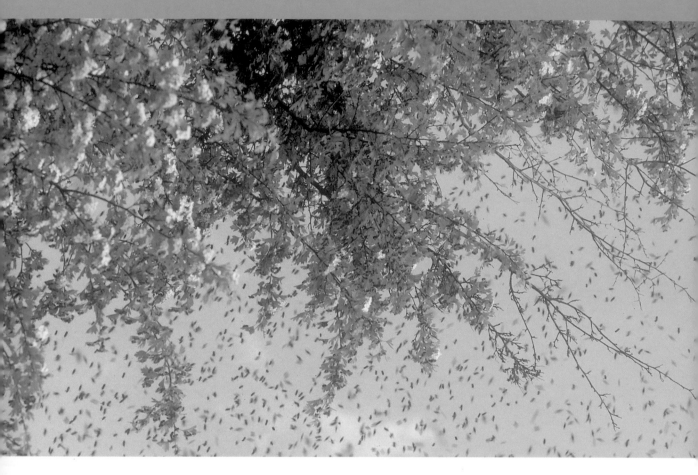

Some eggs **hatch** into princess bees. When there are too many bees in a nest the old queen takes a **swarm** to find a new nest. A princess becomes the new queen.

Gardeners like worker bees because they take **pollen** from flower to flower. This makes new seeds for new plants. Many people like to eat the honey that bees make.

How are bees special?

Bees have long hairs on their back legs which work like baskets. They put **pollen** from flowers into the baskets. Their legs look like yellow balloons!

Bees do a special flying dance to show other bees where there are lots of flowers. Sometimes they dance in a shape like the number 8.

Thinking about Bees

This honeybee is covered with pollen!

Where do you think this bee is going to take the pollen? What are some things that might happen to the pollen?

This person is collecting honeycomb to make honey from the beehive. Why do you think beekeepers wear gloves and a veil?

Bee Map

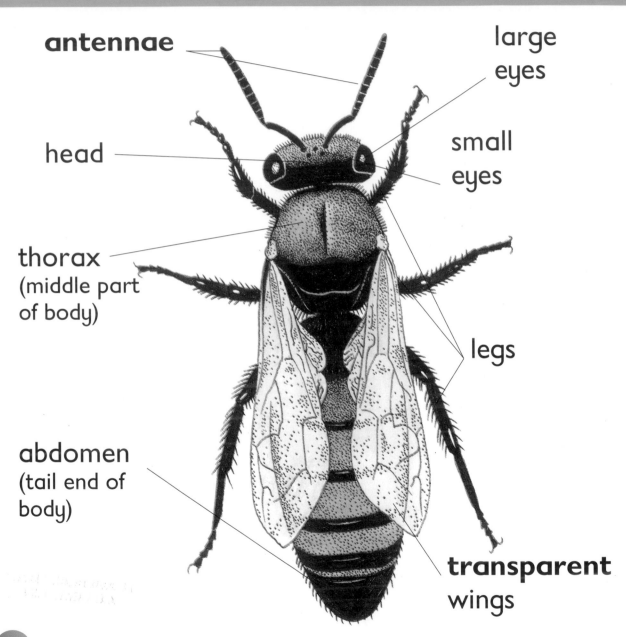

antennae

large eyes

head

small eyes

thorax
(middle part
of body)

legs

abdomen
(tail end of
body)

transparent
wings

Glossary

antenna (more than one are called **antennae)** two long narrow tubes that stick out from the head of an insect used to feel, smell, or even hear.

drone a male bee

hatch to be born out of an egg

hibernate a very long sleep some animals have that lasts all winter

hollow a hollow tree is usually a dead tree and the trunk is empty inside

insect a small animal with six legs

larva (more than one are called **larvae)** the grub that hatches from the egg

mate male and female bees come together to make baby bees

nectar a sweet juice inside flowers

pollen a golden dust inside flowers

pupa (more than one are called **pupae)** the step between larva and adult

sting hurting an animal or insect by pricking it with a part of the body that is like a pin

swarm hundreds of bees all flying together to find a new nest

transparent something we can see through clearly

More Books to Read

Hawcock, David B. *Bee*. New York: Random House Books for Young Readers. 1994
Lunn, Carolyn. *A Buzz is Part of a Bee*. Danbury, CT: Children's Press. 1990.

Index